The Crash Course Guide to Catholic Homeschooling

Patrice Fagnant-MacArthur

ISBN: 979-8-6343-7397-3

Today's Catholic Homeschooling
P.O. Box 81064
Springfield, MA 01138

TodaysCatholicHomeschooling.com

The Crash Course Guide to Catholic Homeschooling

Welcome to Catholic Homeschooling

Maybe you have always wanted to homeschool or perhaps you have been thrown into it by life circumstances. Either way, I want to welcome you to this wonderful, challenging world. You may be wondering if you can actually do this. I am here to tell you that you can. The truth is that you have already been homeschooling since the time your children were born or the moment that they came into your life as an adopted child.

We teach our children all the time. They learn by watching us and through the environment that we create for them in our homes and families. From the time our children are babies, we talk to them, pray with them, sing songs, and read books. There is no reason to fear that because your child is now school age that you can no longer help them learn. The world is a homeschooler's classroom and there are resources available to help your child learn any subject that interests him or her.

This book is designed to provide a crash course in Catholic homeschooling. It will touch on the basics of what you need to know to feel confident as you embark on this new chapter of your parenting life. As you continue on your homeschooling journey, you will learn new things and adjust your approach. Life is always changing. Like our children, we are always learning.

The most important first step in homeschooling, as in parenting in general, is to ask God for help. I can't imagine homeschooling without God's assistance. I pray every day that my children learn what they should. When I've had particular struggles on my homeschooling journey or have been trying to discern next steps, I pray for those specific intentions. I invite you to do the same.

With God's help, you can do this. Welcome to the journey!

How Do I Get Started?

If your child is currently enrolled in a public, private, or charter school, but your child is home due to a long-term school closure, you don't need to file any official paperwork.

If, on the other hand, you are looking to formally homeschool your child so that he or she is not enrolled in any official school, you will need to file paperwork with your local school department. If your child is currently enrolled in school, you will need to withdraw him or her with the school office and/or school department.

While homeschooling is legal in all 50 states, each state establishes its own rules and regulations. I always recommend that homeschoolers join the Homeschool Legal Defense Association (hslda.org). They provide a wealth of information on homeschooling law and what is expected in each state. I also consider them to be homeschooling insurance. If you run into any legal trouble with your local school district or with child protective services due to homeschooling, they will offer advice and intercede on your behalf. In my twelve years of homeschooling, I've only had to call them once, but I am glad that they were there.

Common materials that your local school district may ask you to provide when you send an intent to homeschool letter are a list of subjects you plan to cover and books and materials that you plan to use. Notice the key word "plan" in that sentence. Many times, what I end up doing for my homeschool ends up looking far different that what I planned for when filling out the paperwork. This is not intentional. I do send in what I plan on doing, then life happens and my plans change. Homeschooling is flexible. Do not feel that you need to slavishly adhere to the plan that you submit prior to the school year.

I also recommend that you connect with a homeschooling group. There are many groups on Facebook for Catholic homeschoolers. There also may be local groups that you can connect with. It is important for you to be able to connect with other homeschooling parents and for your children to have other homeschooled friends.

What Type of Education Should I Provide My Child?

Maybe you have never thought about your educational philosophy. Many people never do. I invite you to now take the opportunity to reflect on what and how you would like your child to learn. One of the gifts of homeschooling is the ability to choose the methods and curriculum you use to educate your child. Your homeschool does not need to look anything like your local traditional school.

You should also take some time to consider how your child learns best. What is he or she interested in? Does he learn best sitting and reading, watching a video, or doing hands-on projects? Does she learn best when her body is active? What subjects does he or she enjoy more than others?

There is no one right way to homeschool and you can help your child have a successful future regardless of what method that you choose. You are also not trapped into one method. Homeschoolers often take bits and pieces from various philosophies as they work to discover what works with a particular child at a particular age.

Here are some questions to consider:

1) Would you like your child to have a traditional education, similar to the one provided in your local public or Catholic school?

2) Are you attracted to classical learning which focuses on developing theological, intellectual, and moral virtues? Do you want your children to learn to use logic? Would you like them to have a solid footing in the Greco-Roman and Western tradition?

3) Do you want your children to spend a lot of time outdoors and to learn from nature?

4) Do you believe that your children can learn a great deal on their own? Do you want them to follow where their passions take them?

5) Would you like to teach a number of academic subjects while focusing on a particular topic?

Here are some of the popular homeschool philosophies that you may hear people referring to:

School at Home

Many homeschoolers start with this method simply because it is the educational model most of us are familiar with. It basically tries to replicate the traditional school day at home with set subjects and a set schedule. Users of this method may employ an "out-of-the-box" curriculum which includes all you need for a given grade level.

Classical

A classical education focuses on developing theological, intellectual, and moral virtues. It looks to the roots of education in the Greek and Roman civilizations and is based on seven liberal arts designed to develop thinking skills. The *Trivium* of grammar, logic, and rhetoric provides the tools of language. The *Quadrivium* focuses on arithmetic, geometry, astronomy, and music. Latin is also usually studied as it is the root structure of many languages and is the traditional language of the Catholic Church.

Charlotte Mason

Charlotte Mason (1842-1923) was an Anglican British educator who pushed for a shift from a utilitarian education to one based on living ideas. She wrote *The Ambleside Geography Books* and six volumes on education as well as a study of the life of Jesus. Her philosophy centers on respecting children from the time that they are born, the use of living books written by one person with a passion for the topic as opposed to multi-authored textbooks, narration, habit training, and relatively short lessons.

As Mason was Protestant, Catholic homeschoolers who use her methods tend to incorporate our own religious outlook and tradition.

Montessori

Maria Montessori (1870-1952) was an Italian Catholic physician and educator known for her work with mentally disabled children. She later adopted her methods for use with all children. Hallmarks of this method include the use of child-sized materials, the value of movement, allowing a child to have some choice over activities in their lives, the importance of collaborative learning, use of hands-on learning, and a well-ordered and prepared environment.

Unit Studies

Unit studies approach a given topic from the perspective of several different disciplines. Literature, history, art, music, math, and science can all be taught in this way, with various amounts of each depending on the subject and the age of the students. They tend to include hands-on activities. Unit studies can be useful for teaching several ages together because each child can approach the topic at their personal academic level.

Unschooling

Deeply influenced by the works of American educator John Holt, unschooling is child-led learning and learning from life. It stems from the belief that real learning only takes place when a child has a personal desire to study a subject or learn a skill. Most unschooling parents work very hard to create an educationally rich environment that sparks investigations into a variety of topics. Strewing, or making books and materials readily available to encourage learning, is a popular aspect of this method. Unschooling does not rule out the use of traditional classes or textbooks provided it is what the child wants.

Eclectic and/or Relaxed

As the name suggests, these homeschoolers are flexible and pick and choose what method works best for their individual children. Some trial and error is involved with this method, but many veteran homeschoolers end up in this category by default simply because they have tried different approaches over the years and have discovered that what works with one child does not necessarily work with all.

How Do I Pick a Curriculum?

There is an old adage that says that all you need to homeschool successfully is love and a library card. As I write this during the Covid-19 pandemic, all my local libraries are closed. So I am going to update that saying to all you need to homeschool successfully is love and a library card or internet access. We are fortunate to live in a time in which the world's knowledge is available at our fingertips.

The simple truth is that you don't need a lot of fancy materials to homeschool, especially when your children are young. You need to play with them. You need to read to them and help them learn how to read and write. You need to help them learn basic math. You need to answer the questions that they ask you. If you don't know the answers, you can look them up. A great deal about science can be learned from observing nature and doing simple experiments in your kitchen. Much history and geography can be learned from reading about past times, people, and places. Let your children be creative and explore various art materials.

You can also take advantage of community classes. Libraries often have story times and other educational programs. There are programs for art, music, theater, chess, sports, scouts, etc. Anything that traditionally educated children can take part in after school is open to homeschooled children. Many organizations and museums also offer classes especially for homeschoolers.

Many homeschoolers also take part in co-ops or hybrid schools. A co-op can be as simple as two or three families getting together for a particular activity to organizations that are almost school-like in their structure. Parents are usually required to be involved in some capacity. A hybrid school meets two or three times a week and professional teachers may be involved. The students then learn at home on the other days. Upper-level high school students can often enroll as dual-enrollment students at community colleges. There are many opportunities for our children to learn with others.

Depending on your educational philosophy and your comfort with creating your own curriculum, you may feel better using curriculum that someone else has put together. There are full homeschool academies that you can enroll in that will handle all subjects and provide you with a report card. There are also countless programs where you can buy materials for a particular subject. Big box stores and bookstores also often sell educational workbooks that can provide a solid, inexpensive foundation for homeschooling.

Many of the websites on the resource list below offer free samples of their material. I encourage you to check them out. If you have friends that homeschool, you can ask to see what materials they use. Ultimately, it will take some trial and error to find what works for your child. What works for one child in your family may not work for another. Don't be afraid to set a curriculum aside if it is not working and try something new.

Also, please don't feel that you need to use all Catholic materials. While you can certainly choose to, there are many secular resources that can be excellent to use. The only area in which you definitely want to use Catholic resources is in teaching the faith.

Be patient with yourself and with your children. You will eventually find the right materials for your family.

Resource List

Please note that inclusion in this resource list does not imply endorsement. This is also not an exhaustive list. Please use it as a starting point to investigate homeschool options for your child.

Homeschool Academies

Angelicum Academy
Literature based comprehensive Catholic homeschool program with emphasis on Great Books at the high school level.
angelicum.net

Kolbe Academy Home School & Online Academy
Incorporates classical educational theory and Ignatian methodology
kolbe.org

Memoria Press Academy
Online Christian classical education / also offers classical materials for use at home
memoriapress.com

Mother of Divine Grace
Classical at-home Catholic education
motherofdivinegrace.org

Our Lady of the Rosary
Traditional Catholic education at home
olrs.com

Our Lady of Victory
Traditional Catholic education at home
olvs.org

Queen of Heaven Academy
Online classical Catholic education for grades 4 – 12
queenofheavenacademy.org

Regina Caeli
Classical hybrid education in the Catholic tradition
rcahybrid.org

Rolling Acres School
Catholic classical liberal arts online academy
www.rasonlineacademy.com

St. Thomas Aquinas Academy
Liberal arts education for the Catholic family
staa-homeschool.com

Seton Home Study School
Offers both traditional at-home Catholic materials and online classes
setonhome.org

Veritas Christi High School
Online Catholic special needs high school
veritaschristi.com

Multi-Subject Curriculum Materials/ Classes

Catholic Heritage Curricula
Materials and lesson plans for solid, complete, family-friendly Pre K – 12 Catholic education
chcweb.com

Catholic Schoolhouse
Designed primarily for group meetings held once a week / classical approach
catholicschoolhouse.com

Classical Academic Press
Materials and online classes for classical education
classicalacademicpress.com

Classically Catholic Memory
Memory work program focusing on religion, Latin, history, science, math, timeline, and great works
ccmemory.com

Homeschool Connections
Live and recorded classes for Catholic middle and high school homeschoolers
homeschoolconnectionsonline.com

Mater Amabilis
A Charlotte Mason curriculum for Catholics
materamabilis.org

The above sources also offer many quality curricular options for individual grade levels and subjects that can be purchased separately. The following lists include materials offered independently of those options.

Preschool

ABCatholic
DVDs, CDs, books, dolls and much more designed to touch the lives of little children with the faith
abcatholic.com

Catholic ABC's
Twenty-six lessons, one for each letter of the alphabet with craft, bible verse, and saint of the week
catholicicing.com

Little Saints
Manual includes bible stories, saints and feast days, illustrated literature, poetry, learning games, songs, and art projects.
catholicpreschool.com

Art

Art Achieve
Art lessons inspired by art from around the world
artachieve.com

The Animation Course
Online drawing and animation course
theanimcourse.com

Foundations in Architecture
Architecture courses for grades K – 12
fiaacademy.com

Foreign Languages

Duolingo
Free online language learning program. Many languages available.
duolingo.com

Learnables
High school classes in Spanish, French, German, Chinese, Hebrew, and Russian.
learnables.com

Rosetta Stone for Homeschool
Self-paced interactive complete language-learning experience. Many languages available
rosettastone.com/homeschool

History

Connecting with History
Integrated history and literature-based program designed to be used with entire family.
rchistory.com

The Story of Civilization
www.tanhomeschool.com

Bethlehem Books
Historical Fiction and Biography
Bethlehembooks.com

Language Arts – Handwriting

Handwriting Without Tears
Complete handwriting curriculum for both print and cursive
lwtears.com/hwt

Language Arts – Literature

Catholic Teen Books
Exciting, well-crafted books that raise the heart and mind to God and reflect the fullness and beauty of the Catholic faith
catholicteenbooks.com

Excellence in Literature
Classic literature study guides for grades 8 - 12
excellence-in-literature.com

Language Arts – Reading

All About Reading
Complete, phonics-based reading program
allaboutlearningpress.com

Hooked on Phonics
Phonics-based learn-to-read program
hookedonphonics.com

Little Angel Reader Catholic Phonics Series
Phonetic readers and coordinated workbooks
stonetabletpress.com

Phonics Tutor
Teaches students common sounds for an extended set of
Orton-Gillingham phonograms with spelling rules. Includes
CD-Rom and workbooks
phonicstutor.com

Progressive Phonics
Free program for teaching phonics and reading
progressivephonics.com

Language Arts – Spelling

All About Spelling
Multi-sensory program teaches spelling through sight, sound, and touch
allaboutlearningpress.com

Phonetic Zoo
Phonics-based program uses auditory input to ensure correct spelling of each word is absorbed by the brain.
iew.com

Touch Type Read and Spell
Multi-sensory course that teaches touch-typing skills to help improve reading and spelling
readandspell.com/us

Language Arts – Writing

Brave Writer
Self-teaching guides and online classes
bravewriter.com

Cover Story Writing
Takes middle school students on a guided tour through the universe of story through the process of creating content for their own magazine
coverstorywriting.com

Institute for Excellence in Writing
Workbooks and online classes
iew.com

One-Year Adventure Novel
Guides grades 8 – 12 through the process of writing a structured, compelling adventure novel over the course of one school year
oneyearnovel.com

Writing Strands
Complete language arts program
Writing-strands.com

Math

HomeschoolMath.net
Free worksheets on math topics from addition to pre-algebra
homeschoolmath.net

Life of Fred
Each math text is written in the style of a novel with a humorous story line. For 1st – 12th grade.
lifeoffred.com

Kahn Academy

Any topic you would want to learn about in math is covered on this free site.

khanacademy.org

Math Mammoth

Workbooks for grades 1 – 12 available as downloads or print versions

 mathmammoth.com

Math-U-See

Four-step approach to learning math including videos, manipulatives, writing and talking through concepts

mathusee.com

Singapore Math

K – 8 curriculum focused on problem solving with pictures and diagrams.

singaporemath.com

Teaching Texbooks

Combined text and computer program for 3rd grade – pre-calculus .

teachingtextbooks.com

Music

Catholic Hymn Study

Learn traditional Catholic hymns or chants

traditionalcatholicliving.com

Hoffman Academy
Free online piano lessons
hoffmanacademy.com

Making Music Praying Twice
Fun and faithful Catholic music program for young children designed to increase music aptitude
makingmusicprayingtwice.com

Piano Nanny
Free online piano lessons
pianonanny.com

Religion

CatechismClass.com
Online classes for children and adults
catechismclass.com

Didache Series for High School
Presents life and doctrine of Catholic Church utilizing Catechism, Scripture, saints, and Doctors and Fathers of the Church
theologicalforum.com

Faith and Life Catechetical Series
For grades 1 - 8.
ignatius.com/promotions/faithandlife/

The Story of the Bible and Catholic Courses
tanhomeschool.com

Vision Books Lives of the Saints
Biographical chapter books for ages 9 - 12
www.ignatius.com/Vision-Books-C1091.aspx

Science

ACS Middle School Chemistry
Free downloadable lesson plans
middleschoolchemistry.com

The Homeschool Scientist
Experiment ideas, curriculum choices, and science resources
thehomeschoolscientist.com

Home Science Tools
Lab kits and science supplies
hometrainingtools.com

NASA Science Resources
Weather and meteorology
scijinks.jpl.nasa.gov
Space
spaceplace.nasa.gov

What if My Child has Special Needs?

Homeschooling a child with special needs can be an extra challenge, but it can also be an extra blessing. While there are certainly many caring special-needs professionals within the school system, there are times when working one-on-one with your child at home can provide them with the attention they need to thrive. Children with ADD or ADHD may also benefit from the ability to move more during the day.

I have some experience with teaching children who learn differently. My oldest son has high functioning autism. My second son is gifted in math but has dysgraphia (difficulty with written expression). My daughter is adopted and has some trauma-related behaviors as well as difficulty with auditory processing and reading. While homeschooling has been a challenging road, I am so thankful for the opportunity it has provided me to adapt my children's education so that each child could experience learning in a less-stressful environment than the traditional classroom.

While the scope of this "crash-course" book does not allow for a full treatment of homeschooling with special needs, I hope to provide some basic support for some of the more common special needs. Whether your child is officially diagnosed or not, if your child exhibits some of these characteristics, it can be worth looking at resources dealing with that special need. Education is power and the more tools we have in our toolbox to parent our children, the more we can help them learn and thrive.

ADD/ADHD

Children with ADD can often look like they are paying attention but are frequently lost in their own thoughts and may struggle with completing work. Children with ADHD are commonly thought of as hyperactive. They are high-energy and usually moving in some way. They may be impulsive and have difficulty sleeping. They may have the ability to hyper-focus on a task they are interested in but refuse to do work that has been assigned.

Homeschooling a child with ADD or ADHD may require you to work by their side much of the time to help keep the child on task. Starting the day with physical activity can be a huge help. It is also beneficial to have frequent breaks and allow the child opportunities to move. Incorporating physical activity into lessons can also be a help (such as throwing a ball or jumping up and down while learning math facts). Allowing children to play or draw while being read to can also help them retain information.

While not especially geared to homeschooling, I have found additudemag.com to be a wonderful resource for parenting children with ADD/ADHD.

Autism

Children on the autism spectrum have difficulty with communication and social cues. Those with high-functioning autism may be highly verbal and have almost encyclopedic knowledge about their topics of interest. Those at the lower levels may be non-verbal. Children with autism often have sensory sensitivity and may experience meltdowns when they are experiencing stress.

Homeschooling the Child with Autism: Answers to the Top Questions Parents and Professionals Ask is a very helpful book for anyone considering homeschooling a child with autism. Written by Patricia Schetter and Kandis Lighthall, two teachers with Master's degrees and expertise in special needs, it explores different teaching strategies, transitioning back into a traditional school environment or into college and preparing for life after school. They also offer suggestions for dealing with executive functioning difficulties and managing meltdowns.

Dyslexia

Dyslexia may manifest itself in difficulty learning to speak, read, write, spell, and memorize math facts. It is a neurological difference in how the brain processes language. If your child has difficulty learning to read and write, using an Ortan-Gillingham based program can be a great help.

Homeschoolingwithdyslexia.com is an invaluable resource for anyone who is parenting and/or teaching a child with dyslexia.

Dysgraphia

Dysgraphia is difficulty in written expression. Children with dysgraphia may read and speak very well but have great difficulty getting their thoughts out of their brain and onto paper or a computer screen. Asking a child with dysgraphia to write something may lead to strong emotional reactions in that child. While it is important for children to learn to write, it may be helpful to teach children keyboarding (an important life skill for everyone today) to help ease the physical challenge of writing. Using speech to text programs is also an option. Have children answer questions orally as much as possible.

Dyscalculia

Children with dyscalculia have a hard time understanding numbers and math. They may struggle with learning math facts, doing math operations, telling time, and making change. Technology can help individuals with dyscalculia be able to function in the world.

Gifted and/or Twice-Exceptional (2-E)

Gifted children have an advanced understanding of the world in some area. Some children are gifted in an individual subject area or areas; others may be gifted artistically, musically, or emotionally. It is rare for a child to be gifted across all areas, however. Many of these children have asynchronous development meaning that while they excel in one or more areas, they struggle greatly in another (leading to the term twice-exceptional). One of the best resources I have found for help parenting gifted or 2E children is notsoformulaic.com.

Seeking Help

Homeschooling does not mean that you cannot seek outside help. If you have a child with special needs, outside specialists such as behavioral counselors, occupational therapists, reading specialists, speech-language pathologists, etc. can be of great help. If you feel you and your child could use some extra help, you can start by speaking with your pediatrician. HSLDA.org also has special needs specialists available for you to confer with to develop a plan of action for your child. The goal is to have both you and your child have a positive homeschooling experience.

How Can I Possibly Homeschool High School?

I started homeschooling when my older two boys were in second and first grade. Even then, people would ask me, "You don't plan to homeschool all the way through high school, do you?" At that time, I'd shrug my shoulders and give an honest reply. "I don't know. We're taking this year by year."

That answer worked great until my oldest son was fast approaching ninth grade when I had to face the question head on. What were we going to do about high school, and more importantly, what did God want us to do? I did what I always do in these types of situations – I hit my knees in prayer and offered a 54-day novena for the wisdom to make the right decision.

In conjunction with my son, we decided to continue homeschooling for high school, but increased the number of classes he took at a local acting school so that he would have more social interaction with other teens and independent time out of the house. He graduated last year and is now working and living on his own.

That same year, we decided to enroll our second son who was starting eighth grade in a new alternative school on a part-time basis. He attended two days a week and did the rest of his classes at home. After two years, he decided he wanted to go back to homeschooling full-time. We did that for one year. In his junior year, he started attending a local community college as a dual-enrollment student while continuing to do some work at home. He's graduating this year from high school and is close to finishing up his associate degree.

Homeschooling high school is not as scary as it seems. Your child will be able to go to work or go to college even if he or she was homeschooled. Are you thinking about homeschooling high school? Here are some things to keep in mind.

1) Begin with Prayer

It is important to discern whether homeschooling is the right choice for you and your teen. Every teen is unique and even in the same family, each child may need a different high school experience, whether that be a private, public, homeschool, or some combination of the above.

2) Teens are Often Very Self-Directed

If the thought of teaching subjects you haven't thought about in 20+ years (or ever) leaves you in a cold sweat, take a deep breath. Teens can learn a great deal on their own, whether that be through traditional textbooks, experiential learning, on-line courses or videos, or enrolling as a student at a local community college. If your teen wants to learn something, there are many opportunities for them to learn it. Think of yourself as more of an advisor, helping your child to find the resources they need and to hold them accountable for their learning.

3) Teens are Interesting

Yes, being a teenager is hard and so is being a parent of a teen. It is a time of growth and change. But, teenagers are also interesting to be around. You can have meaningful discussions and debates with teenagers especially when your relationship is built on trust and respect. They will learn things you've never been exposed to and will often be very willing to share that knowledge. While homeschooling any age provides the opportunity to constantly learn new things, homeschooling teens takes that to a whole new level.

4) High School Can be Tailored to the Student

While one of the hallmarks of homeschooling at any level is that it can be adapted to the individual learner, high school provides a unique opportunity to customize an education. Most teens have some idea of what they are interested in and what career they might like to have. While you will want to check into any requirements that your state requires, coursework can be customized to fit those goals. Teens may also be able to take advantage of sports and other extracurricular activities through your local high school. Check with your local school department.

5) Keep Good Records

One thing you will want to do as is keep good records of what your homeschooling teen has accomplished so that they have a transcript for college or employment opportunities. Whether you do formal classes or a have a more relaxed style, you can create a transcript for your child. HSLDA has some information on their website at www.hslda.org/highschool/academics.asp while a search for transcript templates online will offer many options for either arranging subjects by year or general topic.

6) It's Still a Year by Year Decision

If you and your teen decide that homeschooling isn't working, there are other options. If you feel called to homeschool high school, don't let fear stop you from giving it a try. They just might be the best years of your homeschooling life.

Homehighschoolhelp.com/ has many resources for homeschooling high school.

How Can I Keep Track of What My Child is Learning?

Keeping homeschool records is important. Many school departments require that you submit evidence of academic progress each year. That can often take the form of a traditional report card, transcript, progress report, portfolio, or standardized test scores.

If you are using traditional curricula, it is fairly easy to keep track of what your child is learning. You will have worksheets, writing samples, etc. to show what a child has done. I find it helpful to date each piece of work my children have completed.

I also keep a notebook which I update each week with a list of what each child accomplished that week. I include outside activities they have taken part in, any field trips we have taken, books they have read, and any educational videos they might have watched. I use a page for each child. One page per week. I group activities under relevant subjects. For example, my daughter takes gymnastics and Irish dance. I include both those activities under "gym". Photos are a great way to keep a record of art projects and science experiments.

If you tend more toward eclectic homeschooling or unschooling, keeping a record is extra important. You may think you are going to remember all the wonderful things your children have done during the year, but trust me, you won't. It is much easier to have it all written down in one place, whether that be in a physical notebook or an online file, so that you can access it easily. It is also wonderful on those days when you are doubting whether your children are learning anything (and yes, those days will come) to be able to look back and confirm that they are, in fact, making progress.

At the end of the year, you can pull together a progress report or portfolio based on the records you have kept. Report cards and transcripts can be created in a word processing program. It is a good idea to keep a hard copy in a strong box as well as a digital copy saved in multiple places. Your child's academic records are important. If you have a high school student, those records will be their primary proof of academic achievement and graduation.

You may be required to or may choose to administer standardized tests to your homeschool student at some point in their academic career. Seton Testing Service (www.setontesting.com) offers a number of options.

How Can I Have Time to Homeschool?

Kids are usually in school at least 6 hours a day for about 180 days a year. Well, that might be doable if you have one child. If you have more than one child and start freaking out at the amount of time homeschooling is going to take, relax. Whether you have one child or ten, homeschooling will not take all of your time.

Homeschooling is much more time efficient than traditional schooling. Many homeschoolers are done the academic part of their day by lunchtime. Do you wonder how that is possible? Think back to your days in traditional school. How much time did you spend standing in line, waiting to have materials passed out, paying attention to explanations of work you already understood, doing "busy" work to fill time, waiting for the teacher to work with other students, etc. When you are giving a child individual attention, the work gets done much more quickly. Older children also often learn to do much work independently, freeing up your time to work more closely with younger children.

In addition, all those other activities that take place in the afternoon and evening often are educational in different ways (it is amazing what you realize your children are learning when you broaden your mind to consider most of living as a learning opportunity).

Another time saver is that you can group children together to learn. If you have children that are close in age, they can often learn subjects together. They might be working on different levels in math and reading different books, but subjects such as history, science, music, and art can often be done together. You also don't need to do each subject every day. While math and language arts need that repetition of daily practice, other subjects can be done two or three times a week and still be learned.

You will need to spend some time preparing lessons. Even if you are using a prepackaged curriculum, it is a good idea to familiarize yourself with what your children will be studying over the coming week. If you are creating your own curriculum picking and choosing what you will use, that will take some time. Most weeks, I spend one to two hours a week on prep. I have it planned in my calendar so that it gets done.

If you can get up before your children, I highly recommend it. There are stages in life when this isn't possible and getting all the sleep you can is more important. But if you are at a stage in which your children sleep through the night, getting up before them gives you the opportunity to spend some time in prayer and eat breakfast before your family gets up. You will be in a much better frame of mind to face your children and begin your homeschool day if you have had some physical and spiritual nourishment. If you are not eating when your children are eating breakfast, this also gives you the opportunity to read aloud while they are eating.

It is good to have your family on a schedule so that they know what to expect each day. Homeschooling is extremely flexible. You can arrange your school time around any other activities that are going on. It is possible for children to read in the car (provided that they don't get carsick). Car rides are also a great time to listen to audio books. Morning has always tended to be the most productive time in our house for getting school work done, but if you find your family works better in the afternoon or evening, feel free to do that. Homeschooled children and teens have the opportunity to get as much sleep as they need. Please don't feel you need to drag your teen out of bed to start school at 7 a.m. just because that is what time they would be starting school at a traditional school.

You can also give your children some freedom of what order they want to do their lessons in. When my sons were in high school, I would give them a list of what needed to be accomplished that week on Monday. It was up to them to get it done. It taught them important lessons in time management and responsibility. If your children don't want to do lessons, it can be helpful to have an incentive. In my family, there is no screen time until the school work is done. You can figure out what works as an incentive for your children.

It is most difficult to homeschool when there is a toddler in a house. It can be helpful to have older children take turns playing with the toddler while other children are doing lessons. It can also be helpful to make the most of naptime. It can often be the only quiet time you have to work on lessons with older children.

You can also balance work and homeschooling. This takes some additional creative thinking, but it is possible. Working full-time is possible if husband and wife are on separate shifts or there is child-care available. Working part-time is more realistic. Many homeschooling parents also work part-time from home, working around children's schedules, at night, or when children are engaged in outside activities. The older your children are, the easier this is.

What Do I Do When Homeschooling is Hard?

There are seasons when homeschooling is hard. There may be a new baby or the need to care for a sick spouse or parent. You may be struggling to cope with your own physical or mental illness. In addition, many homeschoolers experience a period of desperation in late January and February in which they wonder if they were absolutely crazy to start homeschooling. Everyone is sick of being in the house. Siblings are starting to drive each other crazy. Meanwhile, moms take a look at what has been accomplished so far and inevitably feel they are falling behind. One also starts to hear of other homeschoolers enrolling their children in traditional schools for the coming year. It is only natural to start to wonder if one's children would be better off in a traditional school as well.

There's no doubt that homeschooling can be extremely difficult, but that in itself is not a reason to give up the battle. Our call as Catholic parents is to submit to the will of God for both ourselves and our children. Here are some ways to stay faithful in homeschooling even when the road is hard.

1) Pray

Decisions to homeschool are not made lightly. If you feel you were called by God to homeschool your children, the decision to stop homeschooling should not be made without a great deal of prayer. There may come a time when traditional school is the best choice for your children or for a particular child in your family, but you won't know that without bringing that question to God.

A novena to do God's will regarding homeschooling for your family is a great place to start. God will either give you the grace and strength you need to continue on your homeschool journey or He will open the doors to the appropriate school experience for your child.

2)   Seek Support from Other Homeschoolers

When you are having a rough homeschool day (or season), the people to turn to are not your friends whose children leave the house for six hours every day or the family members who thought you had lost your mind when you started homeschooling in the first place. No, you want to turn to other homeschoolers who have walked in your shoes and know first-hand both the challenges and rewards that come from homeschooling.

Every homeschooling parent needs other homeschool parents to lean on. Ideally, these should be people you get to see in real life. However, if that is not possible, there are also many online support groups. Facebook has several groups devoted to Catholic homeschooling. These groups can be a great place to vent, share ideas and prayer requests, and both give and receive homeschool encouragement.

I belong to both a local Catholic homeschool group and several Facebook groups. I am thankful every day for the love, prayers, and advice of these fellow travelers on the journey.

3)   Read Something Encouraging

When I first started homeschooling, I read everything I could about homeschooling. I still enjoy reading about homeschooling, but my standards have changed. I now immediately put down any book or click off of any article that has a "homeschooling is perfect" or "look how wonderful our lives are" attitude. I want something both encouraging and real. Read articles that remind you why you started homeschooling in the first place and why you should keep up the good fight.

4)   Join a Co-Op or Hybrid School

Perhaps your children do need more time outside of the house. If a child is extroverted, if you only have one child (or one child in a given age range), or if your child is high-school aged, he or she may need more than you can give them on your own. Fortunately, many homeschool groups work together to form parent or teacher led co-ops. These may meet for one or two mornings or afternoons a week but offer an opportunity to get together with peers and learn something from someone other than mom or dad. You may also want to consider a hybrid school if one is available in your area. In a hybrid school, children attend two or three days a week while spending the other days learning at home.

5)   Celebrate What is Working in Your Homeschool

When it seems as if everything is going wrong, it is time to celebrate what is going right in your homeschool experience. Does your child excel in a particular area? Do you love what you are doing for science or history? Has one of your children mastered a task such as reading or learning times tables this year. Even in the most difficult situations, there is something to celebrate and be thankful for. Make a list and post it where you can see it.

With God's help, we can stay faithful in homeschooling and educate our children in both body and spirit.

A Final Thought

At the end of the day, what matters most is our relationship with God and with our families. You are your child's parent first. Your child won't necessarily remember the academic lessons that you shared with them, but they will remember the love that you shared. They will remember that you included them in your life, that you prayed together, cooked together, played together, and stood by each other on good days and bad days. If your relationship is suffering because of homeschooling, it is time to take a step back to reevaluate what you can do to change the dynamic.

Our children often have big feelings that they don't know how to express so they act out or flat out refuse to do what we are asking. They may have an undiagnosed learning disability. They may find the work too hard or fear that they are disappointing you. When your relationship with your child is struggling, take the time to do something fun with your child. Let them know that you love them unconditionally. Pray to God for strength and patience and understanding. God wants what is best for our children. So do we. Together, we can help our children learn and grow to be the people God wants them to be.

Books for Further Reading

Teaching from Rest: A Homeschooler's Guide to Unshakable Peace by Sarah Mackenzie
The title of this one says it all. It is a modern homeschool classic.

The Little Way of Homeschooling by Suzie Andres
I've read this book several times when I have felt discouraged in my homeschool journey. It profiles several Catholic unschooling homeschoolers.

The Well-Trained Mind: A Guide to Classical Education at Home by Susan Wise Bauer and Jessie Bauer
If you are interested in classical homeschooling, this is the book to read.

About the Author

Patrice Fagnant-MacArthur has been homeschooling for twelve years. She has a Master's Degree in Applied Theology and works as a freelance writer and editor. She is also editor of TodaysCatholicHomeschooling.com.

Follow TodaysCatholicHomeschooling at:

TodaysCatholicHomeschooling.com

www.facebook.com/todayscatholichomeschooling

twitter.com/TodCathHomeschl